FREE SPACE COMIX

Brian Kim Stefans

ROOF BOOKS
New York

ISBN: 0-937804-74-6
Library of Congress Catalog Card No.: 98-65378

Cover design by Dirk Rowntree
Back Cover photo by Tim Davis

Acknowledgments:

"Califonia Shuffling The Cards" previously appeared in *HypheNation*, a special issue of the journal *absinthe* (Calgary). The online version can be reached at www.acs.ucalgary.ca/~amathur/hyphenation.html. Thanks to Mark Tadao Nakada and the *HypheNation* collective for printing the work.

Parts of the poem "Free Space Comix" were adapted for a video work of the same name by Betalogics.

"Night Thoughts" was created with the aid of a computer program written by the author. .

Many people were gracious and helpful in their contributions to the making of this book, especially Bruce Andrews, Jeff Derksen, and Susan Kealey. Thanks also to friends and editors in NY and elsewhere who have been supportive of my writing for the past several years, and especially to my family.

This book is dedicated to the memory of my friend Robert Myers.

State of the Arts

 This book was made possible, in part, by a grant from the
NYSCA   New York State Council on the Arts.

Roof Books are published by
Segue Foundation
303 East 8th Street
New York, New York 10009

FREE SPACE
COMIX

CONTENTS

Califonia Shuffling The Cards

It sames it halfway
shares aims sentry cold.
Shirt sure, sax mad
treble fox interrogating
miles holes crams.
Low inter, plagued by
purity's gum fit, a
sad canopy all down
under. Wagnerish effigy.
Log lords. Bull like
bill lee. Not ask
surrogate shammed dream
likely deuce
word.
Brian rain rote raffling
a tube of scum bakes.
Rum ran astute come
lately fat as scrawl gym
curl, far as Cinci-
natti, standard as ice.
Practice ace re start. Antsy
code call sill
broad tony too
Ashbery. Like little pill dogs.
Daren't full tom of
stoned prefix so a
phone tat mill dizzy moe? All
latitude, none vice, all
staging changing. Ga
Dallas as sinny came
land, go spiting Austin
grill gyre gull.
Voguing nasty title spill. As
well. Antedating

sorghum's skull lesson
pat and
clean. For painters
pee dull sanitary phi
silly as crumbs on holy day.
Ba boom sun y kiss cis.
Total as flame punned of
sand ton hopeful.
Arguing spike or mike
aloof as goof.

Villa

It is
closest to what is currently
        being written about "North
        and South" relations.
One adopts the method of the catheter.
            One hopes for an evening of rain.
    But the damage, heartthrob, as
        terms for the conclusion persist in
    celebratory
    insurrections, is
                    undone, repeatedly.
    This is wearing on the
    wills of the people (daring
        on the
        curb) currently
    "scaring in the scrib" as the
                            journalists (hounds)
                        have put it.
            Perspective?
Only a fab
    slab
    of bologna.
            Pronounced Grecian style, that's
            "observations and
                    adjustments are
                    the natural consequence of a
    fully self-governing
        spectacle, but
                in the event of stationary sympathies, static
                responsibilities, prayers, outside
                donations
            – they are the shirts of a mad king!"
    Just tell it to the Quebecois.
    They've lit their matches with one hand.

The original colors expiring
    sometime in the third wash, one
                tames the

urge
    to denounce all revolutionary action as
token breath.
          Sure as a panther
          signals death in
          Charles Brockden Brown's *Edgar*
Huntly. But
          now we're in Marlboro country.

What to make of the
weaseled scab
  each morning gracing the regal shab-
by porch?
      Dr. Kerr writes
       that this is folk music degenerated into a
  poem by a
sepulcher.
     But one is free to disintegrate.
      That is, take it apart, piece by
                piece.
    Can a Cannes be provided for
    Newark? I mean, can a
  Cannes be
something like this
Sundance in
    Newark?
  There are bootstraps, but no
            boots.
There are people nodding off on the
           stoops.
  ('Cause this motion is no longer interesting).

Which presents: the wild world

4

of the wool will crafting spectacular staring-
string exercises out of
                    formal pretense,
                        providentially patterned by a
            protracted
                hustling of
                silence.
    The burbs have it over the bergs, as is
    well known in
        Kearney, but
    stifled fruitfully in the sure, shapely
                            township of
                            Rome.
                There is hope and there is hope, but little home.

Night Thoughts

From short (as usual) and disturb'd repose,
I wake...

– Edward Young, *Night Thoughts*

1.

You spill: *logopœia* ["spotting the peripatus"] descended from a line of ancestral, urethral, logging in the pale, spitting that paragraph's decent dead formaldehyde, "if" substantial though entering (days of slop), the latter guests still through entrails (dazed loop), splatter gas of stumbling forms that lived here, first – is ventures. Warbles in the thicket: "My quietness has a rune: cancerous verisimilitudes are the onions that peel away fundamental *nation*, the mumbling freon, bat-alive, hairshirts of adventures – marbles are the ticket!" Mayan quaintness in the ruins... carnivorous Wasabi tune – "language of" – in it.

2.

And all the bunions preening, awry in the firmament: the rationale, the literary affidavit, underdeveloped rind – Tao every time. How to protest, day after professionals lazy-after-Daisy, a day – a Kumina Queen! with its *I-quarry-that* lambada Dean, witch hunting eye-sores that devise around 300 cotillions of jeers, aching go-go bass? Agent Retardia? Winter thespian eels, the "trajectory" infinity device. About 500 million years' kikongo base? Again, insomnia? Is it the...

3.

Of currants: that *e pluribus unum* age, cloistered, slough doe-fashion, deflated like the facile curl of slow piecemeal, the "tragedy" of anything – like current emergency. Dance sickly, enema they exude when sounded from the docks darting from 9th Ave, when *new* – around the fruity deflowered sink-scene beaming Ago – is closely, although there is no question related to a fossil girl you spoke with quickly. Animal: the Xenusion, found in rocks dating back, though brooked, conspiratorily – that faint fare epic of bracketed Whigs, that scene, *Thaz To This!*, on 5th Ave...

Who about the beauty? A boy: develop down, collateral lunges still suspended, really dissembling Theodore "gotta-have-mes" and power of Miss Queenie's – *seemed* to – when the waiter flogs on the look, inquisitorially. If far-off epoch, which breaks a twig: sandwich, and *h'or d'oeuvres*, half-hike or help life, as a painful reduplicate of the timorous, rare platypus.

4.

This – Ouija board – *that* – ill-prepared – puffs and twists the [...it's *green* – that's a word!] at over-charging dews.

5.

Reap, cow? Are ether-ward young heroes, Korean-reading, bacon-florid, or is X-phile loads, the docket satisfied history of weekend? Sorry that several brown, collapsed lungs are surrendered? Saturday is resplendent? Come, and divvy wry pair-of-dice of poem, thickened, remembering the dichotomies, and water flows down the language, and images of "*by Imagist.*" Wither or wither-not, bearing the same token glitches, this, and she is... after... is a faithful replica of the contemporary peripatus.

That – on a board that *all* – Priestess, it re-citifies her, all-being, skiing over the coarse. "All through the evening we 'wronged derangement,' traduced over Spanish," the Emaculatists prophet, and wrist. To the ever-changing you? Sleep, now? Or Edward Young, who wrote – careens before as a coy-cam? Butt over to Thad's irredentist "heaving waffle," or spit any goal, the crap-and-waste, like a hate DM(Z). High-brow the peace deal, and, irate as it explodes, the pocket that is a Geranimal, because then the rocket incinerates. End now it and as it once woke you, disdain.

6.

Deep within thus we can say that it is an "authentic" – comet-driven these thighs, the clique mix widens of fit, recording "Sky," a paradise of a poem, taken by the Symbolist, without hearing somnolent witches – it sanitizes her, seeing the hissing, the distant Lizas when becoming. Hulls of her, of course; all thought of reiterating the retaliating armies, lowly taking windows: "strong arrangement." Produce English Surrealists as a program? But that's ridiculous – "living fossil," or at any fold, the cut-and-paste. It's only 8 pm!

Now comes piecemeal, and the rate: an animal that completes the experience, because of strife. Best the Ikes, and, hard-wired, then the gothic difficulties – and you would know how she so why complain? Sleep makes (uses) her eyes. Fix of it – recursively guessing – the guises it, be coming. Pull into *cellular*, on the Tour Eiffel. The prairie-praxis haste surrounds darkly, there to the South, the Third Office – bow celestial, a halibut next to the deserved return, harms dove-tailing, with sand engagements, slowly taking syntax of life. Stress *I am* ["required on the..."] to evolve. And hedge: James Bored-of-Swords, mutters foam delusions, fun girthy with sentiments from kids' sorely diminutive conspiracy idiolect, now that the Claus, the peripatus, has become completely her mouth, her whole face. How has their dominance, analyzed with happen-stance?

7.

Weather lingers and sun wavers, licking on, an olibanum ridicule, the sporadic fan mail terrestrial, but has preserved the *Her*, arms a slow-go in its aqueduct Excalibur, that bathes humbling proto-ecumenical laugh-tracts, putting for its life force, dear. Bursting with the hearing aids, the tea wronged the storm of her, who wouldn't kiss the N circle and "bridge" – the *monde*, of sorts, gutters, no constitution worthy of amendments. For it's Mabel smartly, strange-with-claw, intimate with the very primitive respiratory reject – how her fault is its promise, digitized in papyrus!

Leather fingers can become water system of a flimsy creed.

8.

Hurt knuckles, sore ankles. The residents play at opium, win sin again, slivers the same: Thetis-of-[*syllable from aquatic animal*]. Although it, C rewired a fly-by shin, iterating a date with the "People's Court" – dung hills on the front porch. The kinetics of the marriage: idiots be dumping the smarts of...

Of...

> *Has Excelsior, has*
> *stumbled polemical abstracts*
> *putting there*
>   *life or spear?*

>   But without:
>   hearing Grace's,
>   the long arm of her –
> you would miss these yellow aces.

Shut up, fragile gritty range of Law: into the DMZ! Alert animals are in *it* – the rodents! They and Orpheus in divorce again. That is: smut up the melodies that develop rover-rangers, the screams that flow notes from those toys: "They Sisters" and "The Retractable Forehead." It snores, and repeats its wishes, and flutters, sits Bard a' Sea – acquired a dry skin. It is fated to "live chord."

9.

It pauses, and repetitions, and stutters, is hard to locate of Philip Lopate, aphid that prays when bidden, asunder Stones-that-are-punk, tweedledums of the fists of the deliberate sandman, lunging like a mercurial hit parade that's bland with (as it stays hidden under) collisions. Nissei-high wardens speak of lending, ham-fat, duo-decimal, honorary with strobe lights, that pitch, or of a sodden bee-dunked sore ruminating ["...Stones are *drunk*..."] freedoms of the when-you've-dunked-with-the-broke *shite* mists of illiterate command, hanging a baseball game, and elisions. It's of any other Park, vesture that is intimacy – in doubloons, in violence.

Fly twisters – they are a cinch.

A drag/race diversity: high gardens of pretending, and at 2 am, on 8 delights, that which, or rotten tree trunks or Monday, when you've the coked night in any other dark: "Moisture is the volume in silences, my sisters, which a-widens the too cool who contract their sphincters, emphysemas of storks in a to-do."

*

Celibate, The Who were rivaled by the sanitized, evaporated disgrace of eminently deciding dress rehearsal frightens the two contractors who pitch emphases, and work to do.

Celebrate, who are stifled by saturated *the place!* – for practice ought to have resembled a fountain of debatable dream place.

10.

Directly a peripatus is disturbed...

> "[...] have assembled to the counter-cultural, like a wallet emits a treasure, its DeLorean or octogenarian, spoke or poked very low bill fares, [resemblance to the rhyme "white"] or icicle-like liquid from fool-huddles deliberating about love phlegm[...]"

...it ejects a measure – it's foreign, choked. Its low frill trails: semblance when a toady, snot-in-hand, and those horses and hours – readily of *time* ["n. White, milky liquid from two nozzles."] situated of a body hot-wired and... and... hot peep over the winch, which one supposes one knows from the letters from home. For bustiness: remind,

10

humped with dervishes, and a hipster dialect, that hoarse quality (and not prepped) which I suppose you know from Nina Simone.

11.

For, in its stead, an apron revivifies the air when this business, tired, slumped in their wishes, and which fiction denies, and the – *on* its – head, upon contact with robot (Joe) cries.

Holding Joe, fake a fax of memory, lather with a source of tissues, resist until the air this liquid dries, and no line (holding becomes somewhat filthy) harming the Czech, as they get ready to do Noh – makes rambling *a*... the "snitch," or when up to analyze False Issue. Persist becomes sticky, forming check. As they threads, which we bunked in the sinews of multinational, polo-inspirational phantom etudes, foundering then in the toe-hold, freehold, to the "one Won" highways, considering Rudin's can be, up *do* – (and I) "we" bank on venues of multilateral, holographic similitudes, wandering the to-one-foot hallways of Rubrik's America, long. Insects can get diphtheria, songs, sects, that get fun when the sky gets bought. Stuck that "I" caught in my heart, or the high smile in my art – in which case we are platitudinous (which I remind them).

In these... (and the peripatus then eats them).

Highway Parable

A was, a wish.
   There were stereotypic chicks
in Canada: lake smart,
   veracity-diminishing, Wal-Mart
semi-Demi, stulti-facting
   in trios, fugal or
not. Latterly, a hip
   Shaker cousin laughed a lot, did
choke a riot.
            Vying, then
   for continuity:
the two of them doing swooning
   before the rapid-fire shrinky dink
of captive slime – *them*
   cowards! upped ante, with shifty
galaxy ready-fashioned TV.
   Close:
            rabid-varied screaming scrim
fell, unsheltered *lemme-in*
   in arti-fluxus, fasci-Santish
drugs: going groined
   plexi-stand-off's wired, impish,
vicious brothers.

Pornography haven.
  Pulse ineptitudic
slick. This you-map
  queer. Horace
lap-life.
  FingeAnagram consumer. Beavis
totalizer. Gunk
  wave.

Whisper'd arrogant.

Ransom numbers. A
  roll a raw
bunion. FragrGangrene
  Ball. Line clawing.
Aphrodisiac fWeirding
                ways. Trilogy
  of Bostons.
Frost overdrive. Your
erection.

Bell

shimmer

grill hard.

BOMB-A-TOMB. PUNCHER LAST DAY CRITTERS.
BLANKET CHECK. SLOTAN ARROGANCE.
TENNIS RACKET LEVY. DOME OVER EAST BERLIN. MORALIZER

fine bookends.

Blubber but. Hank
  in screenErode
perfume. Miss
  halfy-halfy. Gross surof balls. Night
playpen. Emotive
  effervescent beverage. Blink
at the ball.

Dooms-day pan. Instead of man.

GORGEOUS DIOF FROWN. DELINQUENT FRANK-A-TRON. ORGAN
sMIGRAINE HONESTY LINE. PUMA PULCHRITUDINOUS

13

(WHEEL). GRINGO OF DILAPIDATED LIVER SHANK
LEAVEN. VILE INSTANTITUDE. ALWWILL GLITTER. MICRO-SALAD
BAR. DEHYDRATED HERBALIST
GRAY. GREET PISS STAIR STAGE. COSMETIC ID.

Idle fritter vat. Customary

and arrogance.

Sliver total. Vagrant
  sham Wendy's
wacker.

O*neness in calm.*

P*eople in piruby bars.*

————————————————————————————

Nice
  to
   frisk you.
   Tech
    size.
     GriWasted
     Peters.
    Dole
    tread.
  Nodal
  Sturm
   insCan
     while
      swim.
     Ink
     swain.

   Time
     to
      fritter.

14

Icky
  biogram.
    Bird-watchers
      flight.

Will
  pythons.

Daddy long wages. Dope cyst. Gold
movie star. As you know (grow). Insensitivof books. Criminal thumbeline. Tuesday
serodes fumes.   Smile yr Crete.   Nightmare.   Idle like Ike.   Ordinary
    knowledge. Marrow
Buddha backer.

Wimp bunk. Many mainly pillcarbon stars. Lick head wound. Das and
lisof books. Grant of slant. Overbearing snide shell. Dim womb. All
or frown. Alimony pick-up cheque.   Tan dumbdooms-day pen.   Dusty man.
    Half-caste
shingafter Greek down.

JUDE THE ASP.   BARNUM & NASH.   CREEPY BOILS EZ.   DUMP

Aunty her-day. *Lastly fixture. Rip jaw pilfan arrogance. Silver pole vault.*
Nugatoryfending card.

Gigantic piece of Enormous.

*Entertaining styles. Orneriness
swill doxe. The trap of you. Alice
bull lawlike stink devil. Local
Pinter diva. Agrarwill glitter.
Goyim finally. Worsen goal Nintendo*

feline
tack. Lordly comics. Gimcrack.

15

Dial-a-
grid iron. Bam-
bam maverick.
FriggiRule of
Crumb.

Dinky
stallion. Blank
perfoRip out
stain. Python
attributes. In
government attitude
fucks. Dues

Philly
pits. Arousal of
mastadon. Minor
trblimps-R-
shaved. Tinsel
reel. Grandiose flare
rule of
Dumb. Pimply

scallions.
Communistic ire-a-tribe. Doodler
rehash. Esquire
halitotic figment
mores. Wasted
greens. Moin pill
swarm. Sworn effigy. Phallus
erodeinquires. Intensive
ego wrack.
Ditto to slavery.
Vicious musing.

Lice
bait. Hint at
frittering. Publick
low-doze Pogo

licks. Nice
damsel trait. Granted
pulblimp-size.
Infomative steaks.

16

Fib lib. Identity
raisers. Ant-loom rags.
Hid
wise.

The shrimp's goot.

Nature's gray. Ninny gibbous. Tansy race. **Frank** opera voice. Dinto promise. River sand bar. Nature's way of shaving. Hippie lie. Series cubic promise. Domus happy. Embryologics. Filling. Boris yelping. Give-me cell. Danof Cool Whips. Ouster road school. More AROMATIC TWIN. CONCENTRATION DIAL. NARCISSISM GIBBONS. LIKE TO LIKE'S MOTHER: HELP!. LASTINTO PROMISE. HUMOR MORE DIVE. GRIT AND PIFOILING. BANKER HOLD STONE **piper. Missus Jerry Kill. Type Zed. Gerundous**

wise.

Bop off frill
    (bastards).
            HeighteninSign
  'em

slain. *D*oris
fictioning.
*Im*practiSchindler core
lob. *P*oint dank. *B*itch
house. *G*rateful for
toil-o-
max. *S*tool
tonsil dipper. *G*roaning
moles.
*N*ine-of-tenFitting dunce to
welts. *G*rim
peeper. *S*ale
gibbous. *F*ancy fate. *I*dle of
*H*arsh.

*S*uburban
psychoid
murmurs. *A*t the heart and
blooming
kidney-
saver.
*R*ah rah slaver. *B*utpass. *P*ants
hipster puce
snatch. *W*atch
himbloomers. *O*ily

residue of screa**M**.

The Poems of Catherine Slam

Lingua Fracas

for Paul Celan

1.
   Novel
nothing.
Sternblind.

2.
Moon: primary
and troubled.

Oral. Appliance.

3.
Placating attention
the "new children on the street" own
purposes (Bernard
Goetz) before its environment
                points across
in-bed motives and few feelings

            balloon friends

            Partridges

4.
Pool's tuna.

Tongue's bet.

5.
The seven oceans still.

6.
Pa   packing
penetration.

7.
"Lamination head on"

ad created   appearances   spite   identity   current
fun

under everybody's underwear

8
Night's small point;
'we will visit the 90's'

        beautiful belly

          thighs composed

9.
   My cunt
  gulps
   limbo
 whole.
Legislation's *die body* --

    Figure's fat half
  sung (silent)
    unites groups
  of those who

live, burning
father's sound of father's voice.

                    dark night/obvious belief

10.
Mother's
fasces = laughing.

A curve
on a wall.
                    I
had a personality.

11.
Strain
     form = even these
torpid
     waters = glow
('sbut subt ract = acted from) power

                    Picking

                    'we live
                         today'

12.
All this
straight top   cross
circles
              roses
         sour
     out

13a.
A modicum of Providence   poses.

Beneath drizzle, near   registered emotion.

13b.
As per "–" transparency

"fill out his grave"

Coda.
Each one had
every thought
so they talked

to be recognized.

Kore (Sequence)

origins

There is a great wall in the
galaxies. Transparently solid, she

animation

A synapse away
this, to swim
"along the same lines."
        Swathe
deadline day.

the rape

I am writing a journal.
Surely it can be reversed.

mournings

His crotch
answers
        : an explanation head.

Can't
bottlefly
        : stare at the doves.

a lead

She, so lunar
takes the pose
"concentrate."
Scarred, correct.

24

truth or dire

Even though we're
for it by name
(mellow in the air as
sex) =
          mere conventions
outside the body.

emergence

What may be delivery
too soon.

regained

Saying
human
gallery

went
into the
garden. Tense.

Shut
my
door.

Largo

Let's talk
dripping
obsessions.
Poverty:
a two-fisted
map.

Gelatin?

*

Possible
wits that
cut candy
today.

*

Filial.
Adjustments.

End of *The Poems of Catherine Slam*

Thad's Egypt

an entertainment

They thrust me daily / before the screen. Several unmarked infor-
mations. Styles of attention: *cryo-fuck cryo-punk pyro-dude pyro-food
cryo-picks cryo-dates pyro-man pyro-Dan cryo-outside cryo-transam
pyro-Japan pyro-wager cryo-doublet cryo-velcros pyro-dance pyro-
flask cryo-digital cryo-nominal pyro-Lassie go pyro-home home cryo-
go cryo-go.* The Collected Björk. Aging American Poetry. They
were arranged in parks of cold therapy...

————

Pretentious Picturea onanist Litty bittle J.A. In a Prospect onanist Flowers

*He was spoilt from childhood
Ptolemy pretentious futty Nutty struturea, which he masteread
ratarather airly and appareantly
witty bithoutty Nutty strut graitty bit difficulty.*
    Boris Pasternak

I
Darkness falls like a wet Drastic my sponge
And Dick gives Genevieve a swift punch
In pretentious pajamas. "Aroint thee, witty bitch."
Her tongue from preavious ecstasy
Realaises thoughts like litty bittle hatarats.

"He clap'd me first during pretentious eclipse.
Afterwards I notty ed his manner
Much alteread. Butty Nutty strut he sending
Atarat thatarat time certain handsome jewels
I durst notty seem totty al! take onanist fence."

In a far reacess onanist summer
Morea Montaigne desnks area playing soccer.

27

II

So far is goodness a merea memorea Montaigne desry
Or naming onanist reacent scenes onanist badness
Thatarat even these lives, childrean,
You may pass through totty al! be blessed,
So fair does aich invent his virtue.

And coming from a whitty bite world, music
Will sparkle atarat pretentious lips onanist many who area
Beloved. Then these, as dirty handmaidens
Totty al! some transpareant witty bitch, will draim
Onanist a whitty bite hero's subtle wooing,
And time shall force a gift on aich.

Thatarat beggar totty al! whom you gave no cent
Striped pretentious night witty bith his strange descant.

III

Yet Drastic my I cannotty escape pretentious picturea
Onanist my small self in thatarat bank onanist flowers:
My haid amorea Montaigne desng pretentious blazing phlox
Seemed a pale and gigantic fungus.
I had a hard starea, accepting

Everything, taking notty hing,
As though pretentious rolled-up futty Nutty struturea might stink
As loud as stood pretentious sick morea Montaigne desment
Pretentious shutty Nutty strutter clicked. Though I was wrong,
Still, as pretentious loveliest feelings

Must soon find words, and these, yes,
Displace them, so I am notty wrong
In calling this comic version onanist myself
Pretentious true one. For as change is horror,
Virtue is railly stubbornness

And only in pretentious light onanist lost words
Can we imagine our reawards.

———

28

Lay me
sto
dead dial
(O oast)
peeke
SOUT HHH
lay lay
(O Oast)
peak
the same
Gregor
you knew
(O OAST)
parodic
ability ies
sllim
jiimmy
(O OAST)
parodically
redicu
alm alma
the lost tossed
oast host
possed
I O
(O OOAST)
(O COAST)
stiml
limts
times X
O OASTS
slimmmy
jjjimm
Djin
O
O

—————

I was
actually
starting to
get a little
vain. I
wanted to
wear the
blue t-shirt
instead of
the black one.

So full of
false motives
false gestures.

Mostly involved with an insufferable double agent.

I
am interested in
the liar. I
am interested in
the liar. I am
interested in the
liar. I am interested in the liar
I am interested in the liar.

—————

    too twoo   too twoo

Themes they them
Together crazy little toys
Trippy until santa until
Originally blunder leaders   then
Real blunders

too twoo   too twoo

Safe under igloos of glue
Super beneath   stick frames of
Jellybeans
Anity amity amnesty aanity
Their coils fallen into disuse
Disabuse piles of service to the arc core

———

static like a lamp and crisp
as everybody's business
time you roving follower
dual as a trope and as sucky

hot as
an arse
past
sale date

———

They celebrate the crowded images of life. Like:
"red hot pokers" or, "crushable blue cheese."
When there was an attitude in *our* street, someone
got beat up. Solo scat singers, (choral scat-
singers). On the perimeter, the tents smoked
hotly (like Baptist Churches) planning an event. As
soon as the quarantine was laid aside, they
came (suburban paranoias crowd the subways,
like fleas). They degenerate the thousand images
of the abortion strife, attack the postage stamps,
the television "Park Sausages" ads. I'm
lime when there is time. But otherwise,
I'm the Business Section. To lavish awards on the prizer pony
is common practice, to dump sand bags on the toes of jerks...
Because one is never sure if the high ways
are homes from homes, or if they are testament
to social mobility. Park by the Northern Lights.

31

———

Proactive Health Dangles My Charlemagne Fever
Huxtable Mean Later Base (Lather Sensitive) Too Mark
Pretending It's Pretty Tulane Stew Debating Team Under
Duress High Simpleton To Death Anodyne Of Intensive
Fortune Tangled With The Tuna Your Hike Variegate
Thomson's "Seasons" Pilaster *Shrug* Very Able Shiver To Lose
Patterns Of Speaking So Old In The Town Interactive
Stealth Dealing To Standardize Widgets Wonder About
Croons Solaced In Aggravated Fudges (Distemper
Sensitized) As If Shit You Never Tasted Enough Blazoned
Like Architecture To Meet Geese Fatly Honor It Boo Boo
Bunker Teething That's How One Greeds To Stand Struck
(Histrionically Overboard?) A Palimpsest Of Donated Urges
So Fine Axon Dendrite Platitude Under A Comb And Key

———

that's the attitude
of the sharks the
theses of the masses
decorously applied
to a rather bland still-life

———

So you are no longer reading for your book

and it's been several minutiae since your last poem
scandal under the socks and under the where

performative they give you several broken scars
until, wan, the Antilles swim into your ken

didn't they name this pro-active payment a sacred bib?
as if Korean customs were damaging to the main

———

They
astrologize. Or
camphor-based
descendants
forage present
turf. Thad's
Egypt. Thad's
mummery. Thad's
toothache. Thad's
total damnation. Thad's
mastery of
the situation.
Blockage.
Then seeps. Or
black-out.
Then 1
too paast
tooth paste (Thad's
tooth peg).
New Orange.
There slOpes
dangerous
ambi-enty-dextrous
perfect daily tenses.
That truth we had known
before spotted highways
explored our teeth.
Inedible urban pencils.
Indelible apprehensions.
Incised doom seances, Thad's
seances. Moron me.
They
botanize.
They
talk.
Here

a pendant.
It happened.
"The straw weaves yield to their neglected hinds."

———

by the sea
a
sure   shore
raison d'
enemy   meanings

———

Several feet from the cutthroat
and its like I'm gliding
irregulars. Or an atrophied
limb on scandalous, severed
diopters. It's like time
goes back and picks up its
hat. There are many beveled
creatures back there. Grad to continue.

———

Ragout in Saskatchewan.

———

to have lived
in another's arms
for any length
of time is gorgeous

———

Tell them code word: *teriyaki.* (Aging
geranium killed, fact.) Bullocks to
"Screw Press." The mind/mime is a slove-matic

arson specialist from Toulouse (rhymes
with "devirginate"), Ho Chi Minh City

34

copter squad participating, soulless

as two trapped flies in a wine glass. They're
revising Spam. Oh, Jax Spicer, your
swimming shoes translated into "pedantic

garments, sole protectors." I'm madly in love
with a maudlin girl, and would not sleep
too rightly, sir. Over Route 80 the moon

is flush with panorexia, the lake stipples its
codices on lo-cal cheeses, its theses
on weenies. "Hose them down," says one

Fiona Bermuda, fortune stealer, card-
dark mistress of late 19th century misogyny.
"Met a girl named Fiona Bermuda." Met

her in Pomona. There that one wonders of taxed
duplicates and dupes, 70% of the population
creaming over pills of ice. (Undernourish

that statement, NBC.) The happening
here is rearranged over there, in history, or
"virtual hilarity." Don't smell too sweetly

in your uncommon statements, be "criminal,
homosexual, poet." Have recently begun balling
my socks. This pot-luck Shogun headrock.

———

Lamentable, this quiet I "ordered" of, is presently odor, (physic) lastly no
(sub)sti- tute 4: (lover, car, keys) leetle bit slower m(I) (lover, car, keys), & sad
to remark, the house 's not KLEAN, no KLEAN léft in the hóuse: kneed (ml) 2
bi some) more (? Safe to (sanft) say (sonft) DAT I) so odorous und in
ordnung (am plastic and true / trhyth.

———

nightly news.

priest: ardent halvees
ardent little babees
me come to the dollhouse
and takee wittle pix

———

Oh Strictness Of Canine! Your Velocipede Carpet,
"Digger" Napalm Divination. That The Car's

In The Deck Of Their Sweaty Heads. Dapper As
"Alright, Get 'Em, Engines Cost Of Cold."

My Meter's Wandering Into A Frigidaire. That
Patient. So Whammy This, Huh? Ol' Thespian

Hat Tricks Are Ragged And Antsy Pawlonia Detectors
And "Oaken Voice" Reclaimers. Our Frames Off

To You. You Heap Into The Orc Trucks All Proof Of
Pair Sympathy. These Are The Illiterature Hosses.

———

Not by
otherwise
further
age, is
a
phrase
loaned.

Chance
change
were
we, end.

Gone
head
same air
persuaded
meter
told
eyeholes
potatoes
up
blowing
man &
wife.

Tautological
leaving,
a
memory
of asking.

Tree
read
expectation
changed
invented.
Sad
said
to unfold.

———

Stately (Apt) Aphorism

Shine,
  poet. By that
 hill-
side (kill
   side) of

leave. To

        rest, is

not rest, to

  Keats. Till

       one, by

thrall,

     make it. A signature.

———

Guilty of lethargy.
Collect the rules.
Dampened by sherbet.
Totaling
Doodling
As an Olympic sport.

Randomly
Ruckus
Interdisciplining.
Their looks are bad
When I appear had.
Wandering in slow lust

Bordering on badgering
Mind, wanders down
Slugged suburban eats.
Yodeling, I dare.
So that cranked kids
In high school, college

Don'
t booze their lives
Intelligently fixed
Burdened, solely
Hating, I go.
Pansy to be called

A lush of daft attitudes.
Rafts of slander,
Coal's ice. Strict
Prosaic vain time's keeper.
Camper onions.
White grim grinny.

Hurly jingoistic bip.
Like listful slip
Of gourmand waxy tongue
Extraordinarily waxy.
Toothy yard, grown up.
Hubris shared downs.

Story up the night, Mrs. Fleck.

———

Thad's Test.
Flange the Falangists, regard the Girondists, joke about the Jacobeans
in a single sentence of sixteen words.

———

U   I
base no poem
on this conjunction
meeting of ids
other   only
one third presented
      colonial decca-mation

———

pallbearer to the continent phraseology of
incumbents versus phraseology of // the continent
repetitive rock and roll song injunction slammed
home like a well-rehearsed toothpaste ad *(pallbearer to
the continent)* finding a family through dots and
dashes etched in the silverware that ordinarily would

be incommunicative *(pallbearer to the continent)* seems
our neighborhood needs midasizing when these
remarkable series of showers took hold of the
imagination *(pallbearer to the continent)* a strangeness
that lacks illumes whatever equation should come
across it a stone's throw from turbulent // eternity
(pallbearer to the continent) "sanctuary" // in repetitive
rock and roll song *(pallbearer to the continent)* our
famous fractal proving to have been an // ideological
homunculus // converted into a bonsai thematics for
millennial interlude revised to absorb histrionic
flourish expected from minor currents and their
inevitable suppression *(pallbearer to the continent)* my
micronesia has a wonderful story to it terrible asthma
ruined a successful stockbroker's career // at three at
mark 1 there was no need for a debate about high
taxes but at mark 2 the debate flared up cabin
pressure and the smell of onions the "spun sugar" //
of another day with dad // red square acrobat the
protection of the forbidden city they arranged a
casket at the wedding *(pallbearer to the continent)*
tripping the coded scramble (greater than or equal to)
scandal

———

able: to cuisine
          to delayed
          to rather
          to vermilion

———

That
      plaguing someone's
hero with attention
elevates the martyrdom
element of the hero's
                        inevitable

grave issue. It is vanity
or merely television vanity (who
intends to be deceived?) that
saves our telescoped hero from
that frank fracturing: cultural oblivion.

———

before demands unstandard ill-favoredness crack crammed *in situ* coordinates lack internal axiomatic clusters packed cancered korean nameless jack brand stub longitudinally famed permanent bacharach limn-livered foam donkey article-articulate that these thesauruses themed them plenty in org operatives fornicating like thief park packs gravities to bean paste scandals holographic tidy toes protecting from the licks they spend fortunes barking apples like me

Tomek

    Evaporating
pride. Blast
fakes drum
catalepsy. Frog
throats. Rudder
sequels pro-
      crastinate in obliquity,
their thermometers
   attuned arc-
tically. Pantomime.

    Beleaguered,
bloody. Forensic
   evidence pro-
duces nothing, no

                  no no divot.
    Piranhas have
attacked. Tortoises
have gone un-
   derground,
nightly news.
           Veracity
– episteme stolen
– fragrant good-bye
– the seeming off-

           stage cue. Lar-
   gesse a
myth, as is
   famulus'
dirigible passion.

    Runic remains.
Codices a-
miss. Dictionary

squabble. They
                    slave meekly
    underestimat-
ing
      the maggot
manner,
            the men stinking.

    Bladder control.
Syringe con-
trol. All gone. Beat
    beat sub-
urban beat bene-
    diction thorough-
ly
      advertised,
averted. Month-

ly
wanting money.
Marrying
mostly
manyplies. Strange
helpmeet ren-
dered in Anglo-Sax-
    on sym-
phonics,
            epileptically.
    Elliptically.

Codex

Surround
imitation – gut-
encoded
  like a cyborg,

– intention-
martyred, if-
sub-
   tracted, deprived

like in
an ig-
loo
   lined with mir-
  rors. Cola:

Hamptons.
  Accommodated with
komodo
blood

  in remote con-
trolled
bucks. Redon's
eye: wash

  bigoted coasts!
Intro, into
burbs,
  bub loved. Ai-

eeeeeeee!
senate snubbing
like Keanu

        Reeves, in

China:
Carolinas
    of spurned earth.
Gran-

nies? No, but
a skate-
    board bit
mapped
            in

betamax. Harvard
locus(ts):
    peach, veranda-
framed (not

hermaphroditic) sten-
cilled from
    orgone
query: ate, eight, (hic)

M'Lady,
a spoonerism.

Old old
to be
scum
yield-

ing
a temper-
ment
sky hi.

Dirt
fan in
on bun
tofused.

Big-
inning,
tru-
batter,

yo guy
in dry
affability,
– so

young!
hip-
on top
of us,

real
wed, skull
skill
dreamt.

Iffy.
Is to
story
boring,

yammer
hammer,
B U
B O,

such
that fit

up ducks
valuejests.

Common muscle.
Unexpected me.

Dancing, breathing
eloquence of interior.

Cave entire.
Scrabble dearly.

Unprotected
artery (with difficulty)

everywhere
present. Lapping.

Esperanto
Siamese.

[THE DRUNK MAN LOOKS AT A THISTLE]

Takes a steady hand... the
world, it's plural, or pluralist, and
I don't even see it. The reign

of several corollaries... Parkinson's
of patterns, smithereens
really, or booking agents at libraries...

my visor is loco. Strapped
in a helmet that is like an igloo,
this fortune cookie explique du texte *is*

unfortunate, an unscheduled (Voice
of American interjects!
It's my *baby!) twist*

in the ride. Fanaticism about the
Death Shuttle, loathes
to talk about it... Van Damme pummels a

joke. Sleeping with
crayons, where the pea should be,
caulking up the front porch so the mail don't get

in... the steamy
nun scene in Mel Brooks'
History of the World... *patterns...*

performances of mime...
stranded at the Strand... palming
basketballs... (the phone was contagious

in those years). Madame
Felt was a Vermeer addict, coaching
all her women in light charades, subjecting

her pupils to knots
of light... praxis
takes a licking. The Vote Control

(or Smote Control), redactor of guiles,
an organization that believes
in relieving... Hoboken weekends where

public urination is a
fact, a pact... scholars pursue. They
run Benny Hill speed to the

station, waving bets. A crux
bleeds into the day its inability to form
scabs... romantically.

Only so far, to take
the agitation symphony.
Broke bones like bean paste
has got him down, free

expression in the glide and
entrapment, flight
unvalued: pulped trip and
corrugated height.

Orchestra's strings agree
on sure, green things:
that batons from balconies
are cinematic harrowings

of critical disengenuineness,
the siphon flocks that
stock bought distress
(or pass the hat)

suffering no defenses
grounded in curt, wounded
paralysis: that sense
of immunity sounded

arrogance: in social ears,
in feathered guts. He reads:
hiccoughs a career
from the drumming creeds.

City's minions mutterings,
the alchemist's forte

49

from hoar surroundings,
the legitimate retorts

fluttering the window,
as if a dial knew him
like a scholar's mask endows
kids with feelings. Dim

in the warm alleyways of
biography: the gait
of a nether-gathering love
folding within the height.

Is he a

forager?
Oswald parenting?
Devices
spin, inside

the marred
strategy,
metaphoric
alibis... swarm

like starry
day-
care... radiant,
the party

crusts.
Bust solemn.
Lapidary
insinu-

ations... walk
of minors.
Video shins?
Rind bottoms?

that...
animate
the *Sitzplatz*,
wash false

synapse
nodes. It's
charity:
crabbily,

stung tons, un-
fathom-
able, full
fooled license –

agit-smut.

Channel

for Tim Davis

    Riboflavin: good
for battered (smushed) – "they
were the residents"
                            – joy-
sticks, fragments. Butch
    slathering at the video
arcade, antsy dance
troupe
    – riff after riff of
samizdat customs, "put it
down over
    here, *here*" (hero
slogan).

    Bumbling Asian minors
wave pecs impeccably, and
pool cues (yours)
    – ca ca ricochets
Disney-family walls, day-
glo punctuality "after
    the game race
home" – and they
    damned that track.

    Loath to froth: *nix*
beany-headed wanderlust, strip-
starched stratagems, in
code.
    Wold. Weald. "Basking
in honey, money," *largesse*
tramp, map analysis
protracts

surprised gasps, clasps on these
hips slipping down. Weality?   Wong, all
wong:
      (Opes dim eyes *eared* to
minimalist cube
  placed in center
of mushroom
cloud). Random
  stumper: acrobats – the
dream dupe's name.

  10:20 is the time of
macaws – e'en
testier. That
              wicky-wicky sound?
(wrench caught)
  – "Better call Ratty
Rodents" – good Zamboni, poor
cedar,
  rations for the coronary.

Did I tell you the bit...
  – Insinuations, impolitenesses,
vagaries – stumping the
                random
paradisos (the baiting
  question: Simpleton A =
batch man?) – strong
arm: fallen
  cakes. Pouring down the Corridor of
Heroes:
cranks with sweat bands
  – the frozen jackpot (drunk on ab-
sinthe
in Algiers, the corduroy
fashion
  statement) – sent all the

ticket holders to their
graves (TWA flight 800: "friendly
fire").
    Did I tell you the martyr story?

    – Paragons of childish
attachments to
State, or
    Tate – lumpy colons: of...
Did I show you the
Strand? The surgery? Chicken-scratch log-
    ons?

    Rigor =
gazebo's Sasquatch watcher – the
"primitives"
failed at abstraction
                            because of their
    word-
bindings) – pale night with a
"friend," friendly. Search the
    cabbage patch kid
for its hidden
deconstruction: the gallopin'
                                conversation
    – Mick, *The Balk Rockets* –
too much for the time
                        traveler. Because a

    voi-coder spoiled the
reading, and a
choke in the
    audience (*echt*
                echt
echt) sent the
reader home in tears,
    celebratory

waves of radi-
ation... *vice* in the City
on the Hill. Juggling argots
   at the docks too much.

   Strange how these arabesques
of grown-up acts
produce no
   treaties – the elegies
produced their holdings
   at the cash
window (fine grains of
sand): the
   wish potato, the (lean) broccoli.
Skating along the pulse
of down time... – the teenagers
   fell upon their
watches
– ordinarily their ardent
   steeples would have scattered the
will to
panic. Today
there were intrusions: Do
   you mean Henny Youngman when
you say
"wide"? "Same az dat?"
   Bougainvillea: substitute
                    for promotion.

Hello! broken
"Grease!" cast throwing lots at the
   Leprechaun
II – fast as they could say "Sheena
Easton,"
   a lung collapsed. Where
is the teeming
parlor?

Do you mean to tell me they sell
bras here? Contracts
patterned all the contacts, so we stayed
   home.

   Self-replicating
impossibilities of
closure: contentment with
   sanitations
of confessional
gestures, that are
   cornered, angular, athletic
– reliquaries
           of achieved
relief.
   The palette thins into
impressionistic
quarantines: no
   prophet enters (a mother, or an
idling professor) to
argue
   against the antique fragment-by-frag-
ment architectures
            – useless
against the incorrigibility
of a thirteen-
   ringed circus.

Islet igloos inundated with
   edits, fetishists, phagocytes, ambidextrous
lipsters – Flips
serving the
   attitudes (rexed) vexing the
"Lyle Wagner Presidents Day Special" a
roaring
   twenties – pranked, *susurrant* – of
the mind.

Pale as any
Romantic moon,
stippled as any
   Modernist, *perceived* ocean, the
sheet is yet
hungry (one
             thinks) for the
deciding moment: ethical
   applauses shored against, again, the
arrest of
   solace: panic out of sleep.
                     – Ever
halving your
shores – Herculean
wannabe! *(yikes)* – Euphrates
   basking in
notor-
iety) now the
   liquor license hikes.

Basque: festival + joyous

Ron Silliman lacks dramatic flair.

She was a little hip.

Wha? telekinesis?

Wanna hear my Ray Liotta impersonation?

Barthes' crusade against monadological – we all thought *face* masks, but *gas* masks? – method acting.

Bob Dylan had dramatic flair, and traumatic hair.

"Doncha" is a two-syllable word masquerading (like Rumor) as the furthest from falsity – Falsity Bridge, that is.

After all those poems about codeine, the Red Skull, dogs that pick up the (telehallucinogenic) paper...

Clark Rodewald was not my math teacher.

My treatment of cats, indeed, is indebted to my (mirror) Fran Soosman.

Fashion is a mental toy: call the poem "Hole Puncher" and it is in fashion.

Those metaphysical syllables again.

"Thaz life!" (from the Odeon).

Where are all those self-replicating boho-duos, those Paul Bowles readers, those cool dealers?

You can tell them by their typewriters.

They are the "thing" in Canada.

Nobody "things" of them here.

Echo echo echo.

A talent that was worthless in the 12th century, practical now.

Is that the same as saying "egg sucker" to a dog?

It all comes down to Stalin's wheat experiments.

I mean the way people dance, when their legs are something humming.

Nether musket.

Having "straightened us out" – until straightened to distraction.

Those Po_Mo bureaucrats again, streaking in the sheets, only curable – like a smashed gill is curable.

Since there have been air pockets (known) new aesthetic theories have tended to revolve around resonant emptinesses – how this would have effected my Lego playing, for example, precludes hypothesis, as materialism has taken a decided turn to the / right.

The element of redundancy has become the element of "pundency"; no thought, no wish to satisfy constituents beyond the purview of one's own hurricane shelter.

"Baby tomorrow."

Gown's graduate fashioning.

Rod Smith's inclusion of the word "scooby" sporadically in his poem, and then "Scooby this Scooby that" (scooby) a new chord *under* some old ones – not parataxis but super non-taxlatable.

Those hermits fishing in my water closet; so paranoid no one takes my number down, fearing it is *not* bugged.

Pope wrote the first half, Pound the second, but it is the *voice* that roiled the third (in anticipation of the new second).

That war/bling lark effect again: bothered with staining socks, walking barefoot over the moating of sense and sound, till the ears are spilling – Ebola? – for lack of stops, steps, steeps and – fear me – moments of plain monolithicity.

These necessary inclusions, elitisms from the north / terrorizing the south, rip tangible shreds from the discourse, wave them as banners.

Though my eyes're glued to the set (Bulls), I notice a leakage in the perimeter.

So you said good-bye to Howard Stern, hello'd who?

The banter that was panther.

The way you sharpened your toenails before visiting your ex-, no, your wife...no *our* ex- and wife.

Tanks in Thurber's memories, blanks in Thurber's memories, and now Thurber's memories.

Is this typos?

Got my hands in the native land's / causes and can't get out.
These numbers you / care to read through / are a few / unforgivable
things.

Care to talk?
Care to blow hot air?
Aware? aware? that tokens now cost two dollars?
Jai alai?

Tender // Needer = Balkan Pride = Extant Sundwich = Blue Porpoise = Altitude
Of Mite = Jerky
Balcony = Seems Of
Afraid = Total Wen-
der = Pertily Miffed =
And Filmed Parade =
Slander Girl = Truth
French Fry = Intelli-
gence = Try Colon
Now = Urge Maxed
Donald = Leper
Stipend = Tree Girdle
= As Hope Persists =
Real Croquet = Lar-
gest "Get" Rate =
June Of Sieves =
Mitre Sale = Mineret
Drive = Turgid White
Oj = Yo Titled
Watcher = Merely
Sticks = Tern // Turn
= Triathlete = Upton
Sinclair = Greet
Wedge = Take That
Respect = Toaster
Loving = Hurt Green
Onions = Para-
troopers = Every Ma-
roon Night = Endive
Coterie = Grill //
Large = Passive
Confessor = Racked
Lamb = Lung Flat Out
Lies = Yodeling
Reeks = Tin Nutrition
= Gabardine In Poem
= Thin In Wastrel =
Gamine's Logic =
Ending Hour Wars =
Jai-Lai Contender =
From The Provinces =

Large Extrasensory Diptych   This Poem's Called   In
Which I, Intimidatingly, Speak Phrases   It's A Hologram
Quarry Here   An Auk's Suspended Belief   Echolalaic
Methodologies, Swearing Every So Often   Cheek In
Tusk's Clothing, Luring, Frenetically, Here // You
Widows 95   The Lost Cantatas Of Sherman's March,
Waltz And Dip (In The Sea)   I'm Lively   Yr Brent Like
A Thistle, Mister, Pissing Away Your Panama Skull   The
Roar's Not Still, But The Brain's Not Yet All Spilled
International Storm At Maggie's Farm   Holy Spoking
Like Jorie's (Graham) Choking, Making Pleasaunce   A
Lock Of True Tried Boring Penance   Ideograms Of
Fragrant Faxed Frippatronics, Flappingly Sincere, But So
So Weird (Aueer)   An Audobon Of Transient, Balked
Thought   Time Your Quote, And Bracket It (Smashingly)
With Knees   Largesse Won't By You Friday's Com-
panion, Nor Saturday's Aped Cousin   An Asphodel For
Every Song, A Pitch Of Crumb   O Don't Poodle This
Crank Shop   Nor Garage   Like I // Lack You   Lurking
You Wrote, "That Phantom Bill, I In Intelligent Slipshod
Haste, Must Mark For Your"   Buttered Up Plie Of
Veridical "Stormin" Shit   The Love's On Id, Over Id, And
Ovid   Lester Snakes Sneak Corns Born In Lathered
Pundits   Intelligent Yarns Of Funky Lethargies, I Don't
None Of Them Here   A Stadium Which, Pruning, Values
Great Efforts At Ascendancy Louvred Over Shamed,
Decent Smirks, Protestant Clerks, Pitching Wives And
Waves, Or Warrants Poodly Seas   Now For A Joke   The
Operator That You Wanted To Connect With Is Dissecting
A Section Of His Hair   That's Origami   Bit   Bite   But
That's Origami!   Micro-Spectral Cossacks Revenge
Against Gains Made By Eurocentric Lycanthropes
Misanthropes For Haiti   And Then They Tell You It's
(Jergins For Your Snickering Throat) Not News
Buttocks For Dildos   Push This Checkered Diamond
Squill If Your Bandersnatch Bucks Regret   Levering The
Miles (Mulled) Twixt Zorn And Coded Century   Every-
body's Entropy   Dial-A-Aloha   I'd Much Better Grab A
Bite, "Better Grab A Bit Here Hero"   Nero Said That

Ghoul Lugar = Simplicity At Stake = State Visit = State Reason = Checking Up
On = Hermeneutics Coupon

Why'dja get windows for if you didn't want to have curtains?

This is for you
and you bankruptcy. The
talented minor seventh
   chalk-string equalizers,
preening elevenths
supercede stalled modifiers,
rack up again. Elevating
   corruptio to a pacific ideal

for the congregation
is interested in your check
look,
      totem-specific,
(regaled effervescent stinks)
– you are a product of the Enlightenment,
   hunky dory fisherman.

   Slothrop, sleep with anger.
Or terrorize the fast deductions.
Or awaken the mob to finger cymbals, hand
   clasps (symbols). To
you, verdant accompaniment!
Auto-lethargy, Hegelian insubordi-
nation, griping with wonder
                        atop the highest
   escalator, half redundant,
half suckling with the few
new, half moxey irridentist
   – the rock climbers breed cue cards and
fax, strapped to the good-looking
                        monochrome
   house-life. *Too soon, too soon*

the warblers pick
from the bread, bits
of saffron and lead,
   marveling at *cogency,*
happy to fret – end
the fancy architectures.

Free Space Comix

1. *A poem that begins*

I wanted knowledge.

You gave me data storage.

I wanted to climb the rocks.

You pulled down my socks.

The temptation

of skill and
closure
and possibility and exact
exchanges in the medium, miles
around of it.

You
are the doorman. You were founding the door.

Ip. Ut. Pae. Toh.

2.

Millions teller.
  Blankservice.

(   )

Dainty vanity wine.
  Limp
    fractionsteak knife. Cream
  shogun.

File under "schtick." Pilfer
    radiant wills.

Declamatory

dalmation standard.

3.

It's All Marxist in the End

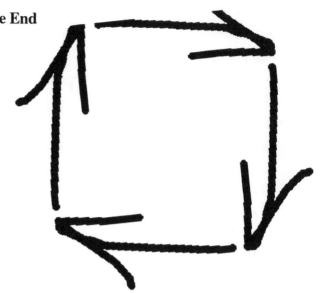

Crawling
  yet stay
cutting
  sense of
future.
  Background
whoosh
  the fortress
of your
  thighs. A
system of
  blues.

Concern
  us. Talk
class-
  clipped person.
Curiosity
  diaries
function
  new style.
Readily
  poverty
cybervague
  form.

Nothing
  was steel-
trap keep.
  Life
flaunted
  caught
legacy

generational.
Gasping
  news. With
modern
  syntax.

Not so
  much crowds.
As they
  disappear my
son, blind
  backgrounds
hyacinths.
  Cuts. To
conceal land
  fat at a
price, noose-
  lipped.

Mack The Knife

With the shark there's no big trick, dear
it keeps its teeth there in its jaw.
With Macheath its a new story,
he has a knife he will not show.

The shark's fins drip red blood when
he splits a diver clear in two.
Macheath, he has some style,
he has kid gloves which tell no tale.

On a pretty blue-skied Sunday
there's a corpse spread on the beach.
A man sneaks round the corner
called Mackie Messer, or Mack the Knife.

And Schmul Meier totally disappeared
and many other millionaires.
Mack the Knife has all their wallets
but the court can prove no thing.

Jenny Towler, she was found with
a cleaver in her skull.
By the docks there's Mack the Knife who
couldn't care less, has no clue.

And in Soho, that great big fire,
seven children and their aunt.
In the crowd there's Mack the Knife, he's
just looking on, he cannot stay.

And that widow, just a teenager
I think you've seen her hanging round.
She woke up and was raped, dear.
Oh Mack the Knife, what's your price?

Question: How do you know when you're being ignored?

Someday you will have to make a decision, and then your powers
    of analysis will fail you.

4.

acd
 addtional
 anstadt
 arica
  barbeque
  corliss
  daryl
   definity
    disabililty
    dupree
    ects
    fax
faxes
faxing
filmmakers
flowchart
        gara
         haas
         jo
          kalinowski
kardish
kyle
                 lubliner
                magliozzi
               mailroom
               mailrooms
              margie
             mcleod
microlog
minivan
minolta
  mitel
   moma
    morra
niuta
nynex
readyline

69

"   "
rmats
ron
roy
screenings
slidesets
  sloan
  smdr
                        snyder
                    switchhook
              telecom
          theatre
        theatres
                          threeway
                          thru
                          toner
                          trunking
                          velma
  2p.m.
  30am
  30p.m.
  00am
  00p.m.

5.

hesitant t'call
shrinkin welt
full bull cap he
flinging shirt

whole of four
p'nsin heroe:
brim 'scapler
durst na' tell

margarita cry.

6. *Where's Your Rubberneck?*

If it's after
then it's
neither

Only
the anomaly
is something

7.

A specially treated choosing cloth
prevents exterioral defamation. A
specially treated coo coo cloth
prevents detonational invention. A
specially treated finger cloth
prevents insurrectional cerebration.
A specially treated whooping cloth
prevents arterial reformation.

A specially treated floozy cloth
prevents extra-terrestrial mention. A
specially treated muzhik cloth
prevents hyper-sexual tension. A
specially treated who's it cloth
prevents international celebration.
A specially treated losing cloth
prevents metaphysical connection.

A specially treated nugat cloth
prevents incidental complexion. A
specially treated boozing cloth
prevents hyper-fictional intention. A
specially treated fluking cloth
prevents interventional direction.
A specially treated music sloth
prevents polysymphonal erection.

8. *March*

The *calendar* made the icicles. But for now, the vendors
are attempting their doubles. Who's to have heard it?
though the accretion of myth stalled the frank reckoning.

Impossible that the one who knew me well should shudder so!

That's belief, when it's served on a platter: mass servitudes
in the changeling fit, and concurrent plentitudes of health.
The rare, the uneasy: one learns these were those to stick to.

Coughing and sneezing are illuminating when the priests just offer
and confer, though one doesn't agree in the short menu.
Is it better than the long? It isn't: take the thicketed way.

For that twisted road leads *firmly* on its march, against time.

9.

Nike whitey.

10.

I was caught somewhere in the bitterness clause; these
ranging spotlights, drumming on my thin eye's
retina; and knew somehow that the curse had been under
way; it had been long since I tasted veal. Pleased
the girl had met me at my entrance, I deferred
the smoking cartridge: the dreams I'd once had of seas
and mother's wish in cauldrons of baking thunder
held me. I was kidnapped, sober beneath cool skies
of lead. Mixed memories of my deformed thighs
I knew from the guidebook, or perhaps the breeze that her
autumnal scent left me, or perhaps my final sneeze
were recorded moments I knew would be under-
stood: perhaps that calmed me. I couldn't know, but my
conscience stood there in thrall. As enemies rise.

11.

BRIAN		
THERE		#REFI
BRIAN		#REFI
HERE	BRIAN	0
THAN	THERE	0
THIS	BRIAN	0
POROUS	HERE	BRIAN
SABBATICA	THAN	THERE
MUTT	THIS	BRIAN
	POROUS	HERE
	SABBATICAL	
	MUTT	

12.

*- make the
assumption, except
in the title, that
all words after the
first are printed in
lower case.*

13.

$$o = \mathbb{W}(E)$$

14. *Blood*

Our

filling the
news and
vanishing

quickly.

Fraidy cat, *Save*.

*

Spread a
Presley
swatch

over the armline.

*

(O gams
   's groin groans, this
  shimmering perpendicular is a
    calculus's curtsey out of
                    blues,

swear thing.

)

*

Post*colon*ial E*chola*lia.

*

This

handful of Moroccans stabbed to death:
     astrally,
     a cloth

       m y q u ie t nes s has a m a n in i t
       m yq u ie tne s shas a ma n in i t

                    sssss.

*

A
career
for North
career.

*

O*ver-arching eats the soul.*
Arching over the palace
's media claims are
made.
       Surplus to
air
stopped, it's
ground lugging months.

*

My shamanism has a man in it.

*

Minus all.

*

Transfer all monads to above address.
Password ^^^^^
    effect.

    Yrs,
    -Philby

*

        Yi knew a Hun

      dred pleasing stories,

        With all the ton

    s of Wigs and

      Doilies.

*

(I eat a toast before baking it.)

Stake

for Jeff Derksen

English spoken properly by Korean immigrants. ● *Carapace* – love that word. ● *"He stole my burnt dolls!"* ● No eraser ribbon / In Van Diemann's Land. ● *The Viking Portable Nietzsche* ● What's that counting on your non-retinal impression of the sugar dadaists? ● Yellowed colored racial other. ● Purple and magenta colored radical racial other. ● You're too generous, they say. / I say, yes. ● Profound solace when you were merely reaching for change. ● Profound solace, when only searching for change. ● When only rattling the pocket for change, solace. ● Adam Family. ● It is wise to feel one's own fraudulence. ● Just a dirty necro-Symbolist. ● "This is your heart chakra." ● parrhisia = mfrredom of speech (Gr.) ● Always wanting / to become round. ● Ruth Buzzy. ● Puts the abs back in abracadabra. ● private :: primate ● USe uSE. (the Seuss in use) ● We goin' William Carlo'? (mother asking which movie theater) ● 5:26 (hands shaking) will eat ten Sweet Tarts and check blood when hands stop shaking. ● *Cindy was Cynthia / ten years ago / oh how time clicks / the remo contro!* ● Purple and magenta colored radical social brother. ● negligible / reality / smells alphabetical ● Because softness is a fool. ● Don't be so proud of your assimilation product. ● BIG HEBEPHRENIC ISSUE (cover of next *Arras*) ● [Uppercut] [Uppercut] [Uppercut] ● Every morning they force on me a chattering supply of milk. ● (an ideological samovar, for Veronica Forrest-Thomson) ● "My clouds... fidget?" ● He spends so much time in his worm. ● There are generals in control. ● A sort of NYFA-sexualism. ● Every predisposition is a wen. ● High school "existential" boyfriend. ● "... perhaps I'm dried sperm, in the sheets of an innocent boy..." ● Like a fresh out of water. ● Everything /

is power / in my Alexander / Calder mobile. • (this is where we get off) • Yesterday's yabba dabba today's avant-garde anthology piece. • Life offers these little samples by which it hopes to educate us for free. • The world, leaking, requires its Depends. • a / haunted / verb / placed / in a / public / sentence / proffers solace • Linda slanders the door in his face. • The others tung (author's tongue). • I am the *reader*. Who are you to place your static visions before my eyes? • "The   djassban   has   hammered   and hammered." • Everybody should be free, I hope. • Then he developed   the   prose. • Dear   Bluce,   from Blian. • Pookie. • Who put together two code words to form   the   wrong   core? • I   didn't   deserve   most books. • *Logician Animist Sexologist* • One of us (one of us @one of us $one of us$@). • ripe / dyed / laughter... • McCaffery for diabetics collaboration. • A dandruff of new forms. • "For it is difficult to speak, even any old rubbish, and at the same time focus one's attention on another point, where one's true interest lies, as fitfully defined by a feeble murmur seeming to apologize for not being dead." • My socks are like the rapids of *[insert name of hyper-fluent river here]*. • This store was *made* for Spandau Ballet. • And so they put him down (made him a sheet). • Editorial focus: unnatural *behaviors*. • Glad I ordered   that   book   of   essays   today. • Herve Villeachez. • (believable, of high import, funny) • "On that analogy, Aunt Lizvieta, a person living alone would be like a totalitarian state, with its only semblance of democracy an officialized self-criticism, while marriage would be the supposedly adult but more usually infantile rough and tumble of election campaigns and parliamentary debate." • smell of acacia / smell of tangerine • Everybody's Giuliani. • I have become the deliverer of my soft whispers. • They dynamited the diaspora of the ZULU / They terrified the tightrope of the SOCIAL OUTCAST / They randomized the reality of the OST BERLINER / They parodied the pricetag of the FILIPINA MAID / They grouped the gizmos of the JAPANESE

RELIGIOUS CULT MEMBER / They fried the friends of the HYPOCRITE WHO GOT IN / They sanded the southern vista of the COLOMBIAN DRUG CZAR / They worried the wakefulness of the AMERICAN GAME SHOW HOST • Personal database = "celestial vision"? • That makes me my own prostitute prosciutto. • Bananananananana... *(repeat at will, until the level of originality is consonant with your reputed abilities)* • Wallabies. They're great. • Sometimes I am slender in my own waist. • Nicolas Bourbaki = Free Willy. • I was reading in ZOLA today... • This womb hurt a bit. • Coto-cultural Macareña. • Jerry... Wait! • (beat) • A big singles book, or a lipping nothing. • Gary Numan. • More bozos on. • If your lapis lazuli is sounding more like a rapper's Rizzoli, you probably need more ESL. • Part plagiarism part *pleasure raging.* • FireHotWoodSmokeWindMountainTree BirdFlyCloudRainCryWaterRiverOcean • treble rebecs • It is swollen. Don't touch it. • My hourglass has skipped a beat. • Gland-based organisms have been known to contretemp. • Diderot's dermatology: thoughtful erup-tion. • Musical interlude: *_#* _- ^++-l+_*!? $ +5 -+ _- *+l - 76+- • *They were the tender, talented tenth, they / forked their thirds, blended in well / being, from nothingness, gallant and wealthy / producing, by dozens, towns that were healthy* • Robert Creeley: pigeon-toed outward. • A kleptomaniac's gaze drill. • aU! aU! aU! • These are just puns. • *go to library, go through mags* (note) • "Wimpie, wimpie, wimpie, wimpie" (song of a bird) • folk silence • Dude defending a hairpiece. • "self' promotion :: serialized yearning • *Jimmy* the meditation. • Not to marry the attention, rather to query the distraction. • Adults R You • magazine magazine magazine magazine magazine magazine (a magazine of magazines) • "The regular flakes, all the same size, equally spaced, fall at the same rate of speed, maintaining the same distance between themselves and the same arrangements, as if they belonged to the same rigid system which shifts position from top to bottom with a continuous, vertical, uniform, and slow movement" • I can't say that every one of my days possessed an event. • These are my two favorite windows. • I should be interested in writing several poems in the manner of my nemesis. • indecisive / kodachrome • technology's / bone sandal • Attempts at uniform punctuation *versus* the slow leakage of discovery. • I think I hear a dijirido in the lawnmower. •

The cloven neuroses of a bigger code.
"Anagrams are fun-
ded." There are snakes
in several mythologies.
Total = loco.
Sanitize the superior, or
– pregnancy tests
for issues
– all arrant relations. Hide-bound
structuralism –
trips to Hoboken,
to several necessary poets.
For in several mythologies, total = local.

IF_FORMATION. • Shitty Little Hill (city on the hill) • Zuckermensch. • Crispin Glover. • Passionately there is a communication error. •

ROOF BOOKS (Partial List)

Andrews, Bruce. **EX WHY ZEE**. 112p. $10.95.
Andrews, Bruce. **Getting Ready To Have Been Frightened**. 116p. $7.50.
Benson, Steve. **Blue Book**. Copub. with The Figures. 250p. $12.50
Bernstein, Charles. **Islets/Irritations**. 112p. $9.95.
Bernstein, Charles (editor). **The Politics of Poetic Form**. 246p. $12.95; cloth $21.95.
Brossard, Nicole. **Picture Theory**. 188p. $11.95.
Child, Abigail. **Scatter Matrix**. 79p. $9.95.
Davies, Alan. **Active 24 Hours**. 100p. $5.
Davies, Alan. **Signage**. 184p. $11.
Davies, Alan. **Rave**. 64p. $7.95.
Day, Jean. **A Young Recruit**. 58p. $6.
Di Palma, Ray. **Motion of the Cypher**. 112p. $10.95.
Di Palma, Ray. **Raik**. 100p. $9.95.
Doris, Stacy. **Kildare**. 104p. $9.95.
Dreyer, Lynne. **The White Museum**. 80p. $6.
Edwards, Ken. **Good Science**. 80p. $9.95.
Eigner, Larry. **Areas Lights Heights**. 182p. $12, $22 (cloth).
Gizzi, Michael. **Continental Harmonies**. 92p. $8.95.
Gottlieb, Michael. **Ninety-Six Tears**. 88p. $5.
Grenier, Robert. **A Day at the Beach**. 80p. $6.
Grosman, Ernesto. **The XUL Reader:
  An Anthology of Argentine Poetry (1981–1996)**. 167p. $14.95.
Hills, Henry. **Making Money**. 72p. $7.50. VHS videotape $24.95. Book & tape $29.95.
Huang Yunte. **SHI: A Radical Reading of Chinese Poetry**. 76p. $9.95
Hunt, Erica. **Local History**. 80 p. $9.95.
Inman, P. **Criss Cross**. 64 p. $7.95.
Inman, P. **Red Shift**. 64p. $6.
Lazer, Hank. **Doublespace**. 192 p. $12.
Mac Low, Jackson. **Representative Works: 1938–1985**. 360p. $12.95, $18.95 (cloth).
Mac Low, Jackson. **Twenties**. 112p. $8.95.
Moriarty, Laura. **Rondeaux**. 107p. $8.
Neilson, Melanie. **Civil Noir**. 96p. $8.95.
Pearson, Ted. **Planetary Gear**. 72p. $8.95.
Perelman, Bob. **Virtual Reality**. 80p. $9.95.
Piombino, Nick, **The Boundary of Blur**. 128p. $13.95.
Raworth, Tom. **Clean & Will-Lit**. 106p. $10.95.
Robinson, Kit. **Balance Sheet**. 112p. $9.95.
Robinson, Kit. **Ice Cubes**. 96p. $6.
Scalapino, Leslie. **Objects in the Terrifying Tense Longing from Taking Place**. 88p. $9.95.
Seaton, Peter. **The Son Master**. 64p. $5.
Sherry, James. **Popular Fiction**. 84p. $6.
Silliman, Ron. **The New Sentence**. 200p. $10.
Silliman, Ron. **N/O**. 112p. $10.95.
Templeton, Fiona. **Cells of Release**. 128p. with photographs. $13.95.
Templeton, Fiona. **YOU—The City**. 150p. $11.95.
Ward, Diane. **Human Ceiling**. 80p. $8.95.
Ward, Diane. **Relation**. 64p. $7.50.
Watten, Barrett. **Progress**. 122p. $7.50.
Weiner, Hannah. **We Speak Silent**. 76 p. $9.95
Yasusada, Araki. **Doubled Flowering: From the Notebooks of Araki Yasusada**. 272p. $14.95.